WAR DEPARTMENT.

# REPORT

OF AN

# EXPEDITION UP THE YELLOWSTONE RIVER,

MADE IN 1875,

BY

JAMES W. FORSYTH,
LIEUTENANT-COLONEL AND MILITARY SECRETARY,

AND

F. D. GRANT,
LIEUTENANT-COLONEL AND AIDE-DE-CAMP,

UNDER THE ORDERS OF

LIEUTENANT-GENERAL P. H. SHERIDAN,
COMMANDING MILITARY DIVISION OF THE MISSOURI.

WASHINGTON:
GOVERNMENT PRINTING OFFICE.
1875.

# LETTER OF INSTRUCTIONS.

---

HEADQUARTERS MILITARY DIVISION OF THE MISSOURI,
*Chicago, Ill., May* 19, 1875.

COLONEL: Pursuant to an agreement with Mr. S. B. Coulson, the contractor for freight on the Upper Missouri, the steamer Josephine will be placed at your disposal at Bismarck, Dakota Territory, for an examination of the Yellowstone River from its mouth to the mouth of the Big Horn, or still farther up, if practicable.

You will therefore proceed to Bismarck without delay, accompanied by Lieut. Col. F. D. Grant, of my staff, where the steamer Josephine will be in readiness for you; and after landing such freight as she may carry for Forts Stevenson and Buford at these respective points, you will take on board from the garrison at Fort Buford a sufficient escort for the accomplishment of the object in view. I want a careful examination made of the south bank of the Yellowstone and the mouths and immediate valleys of the rivers coming in from the Black Hills, and especially those of Tongue River, Rosebud, and Big Horn, and if you go higher up the Yellowstone, the Big Rosebud, giving an account of the timber, soil, and geological formation, also the depth of the water in a general way, and the character of any rapids passed over above the mouth of Powder River. Make your examination as complete as possible, without any unnecessary detention of the boat, and return from any point when, in your best judgment, there is not sufficient water, or any other obstacles to impede your progress.

It may be necessary, at some time in the immediate future, to occupy by a military force the country in and about the mouths of Tongue River and the Big Horn. You will, therefore, make especial examination of these points with this view.

I decline to authorize you to allow any person whomsoever to accompany you except Lieutenant-Colonel Grant, who is a part of your expedition, and whom you may put on special or general duty with you and the officers accompanying the troops forming your escort.

The captain, officers, and pilots of the boat, and Mr. Coulson, or any agent of his who is undoubtedly an employé or a member of the transportation company, and the necessary officers of the boat, will, of course, have to go.

On your return you will be required to make an exact report of your trip, and you will telegraph my headquarters on your departure from Bismarck, and as soon as you return there.

Yours, truly,

P. H. SHERIDAN,
*Lieutenant-General.*

Lieut. Col. J. W. FORSYTH,
*Military Secretary.*

MOUTH OF YELLOWSTONE RIVER.

# REPORT OF LIEUT. COL. J. W. FORSYTH.

---

HEADQUARTERS MILITARY DIVISION OF THE MISSOURI,
*Chicago, Ill., June* 22, 1875

GENERAL: I have the honor to submit the following report of an expedition made up the Yellowstone River, in pursuance of your letter of instructions, dated May 19, 1875, and Special Orders No. 54, dated Headquarters Military Division of the Missouri, May 19, 1875.

The steamboat selected for the expedition was the Josephine, Capt. Grant Marsh, commanding. She is one of the best boats engaged in the Upper Missouri trade, being 180 feet in length, 31 feet in breadth, with a depth of hold of 4 feet, and is registered at 300 tons burden. She had no freight on board, and was manned by twelve officers and thirty-one men.

Before leaving Fort Buford I took on board of the Josephine three companies of the Sixth United States Infantry, viz: Company E, Capt. Thomas Britton, Second Lieut. R. I. Jacobs, and thirty enlisted men; Company G, First Lieut. W. H. Cornell, Second Lieut. Thomas G. Townsend, and thirty enlisted men; Company H, Second Lieut. R. E. Thompson, Second Lieut. C. L. Gurley, and forty enlisted men.

This gave me, with Acting Asst. Surg. J. A. McKinney, a total of seven officers and one hundred enlisted men. I also had four mounted scouts and one Gatling gun, caliber one inch, supplied with 10,000 rounds of ammunition, and the companies were furnished with 350 rounds of ammunition per man. The command was supplied with one month's subsistence; and the steamer with this escort and supplies drew twenty inches of water.

In order that we might make an early start on the following morning, I pushed off from Fort Buford and headed for the mouth of the Yellowstone River, which is just above the post, at six o'clock p. m., on Wednesday, the 26th day of May. Moving up the Missouri to enter the mouth of the Yellowstone, you travel around the arc of a bend which the river makes to the north, pass by the Missouri River, which comes in from the north, and find yourself stemming the current of the Yellowstone, which rushes into the main stream with such force that it cuts off the Missouri and seems to claim the entire right of way, and so impresses you with its might and usurped power, that you are naturally led to believe that it is in reality the parent stream and the Missouri one of its tributaries.

We steamed up the Yellowstone until 8 o'clock p. m., and then tied up for the night on the north bank of the river, opposite Forsyth's Bluff, said to be twelve miles from Fort Buford.

As soon as the boat made a landing, we posted a strong guard on the shore, well out some 300 yards from the steamer, and this course was pursued at every landing that we made, either for wooding up or for night camps, during the entire expedition.

We left camp opposite Forsyth's Bluff at 4 a. m., Thursday, May 27, and at 9½ o'clock p. m. on the third day, Saturday, May 29, we went into camp ten miles above the mouth of Powder River. The average width of the Yellowstone passed over by us up to this point was about 300 yards, and the water was at least 2 feet below the usual high-water mark. The banks and bottom of the river, from its mouth to Stanley's Shoals, forty-two miles from Fort Buford, are about the same as that of the Missouri, but at these shoals the bed and bank change to gravel; and the Yellowstone, throughout its length passed over by us, is bounded by a gravel bed and walls. We had no trouble in making our way up to this camp by the use of our steam-power alone; found no snags or rocks to interfere with our progress. The water was muddy, but not so thick and bad as the Missouri. Current about four miles an hour, except on the rapids, where it was, of course, much greater. The main Wolf Rapids, which are regarded as about the most difficult ones in the lower river, are 250 feet long. We steamed back and forth across them and examined them with great care, taking soundings. The least depth of water near the channel was 8 feet, and we estimated the current to be about six miles an hour. The south bank, near Wolf Rapids, has a perpendicular face on the river 50 feet in height, with horizontal veins of coal 5 feet and less in thickness running through it. The ground on the north bank drops down into a low prairie point.

Powder River at its mouth is 125 yards wide, current sluggish, and the water of a dark-reddish color. Its east bank is bounded by a rough line of hills of a bad-land character and appearance. On the west bank there is a small patch of prairie near its mouth. Very little open country on the south bank of the Yellowstone; on the north bank high prairie, which is quite extensive, varying in width, and is finally closed in on the river by a range of hills 350 feet high, which form the north bank of the river about two miles from our camp, and which from their appearance were called *Devil's Backbone Buttes.* They pushed down on to the Yellowstone in our front, and seemed to be barriers to our further progress to the west. Small amount of cottonwood and willow on the Powder River; very little growing timber on the Yellowstone. The prairie above referred to is covered with sage, some bunch-grass, and prickly pear. About five miles above Powder River, a small creek winds its way through it, and is known as Custer's Creek. Near this stream General Stanley camped with his command in 1873.

*Sunday May* 30, 1875.—We camped last night at a point on the north bank of the river, which we called Eagle Point, and the small island just west of it was called Eagle Island.

Left camp to-day at 3.30 a. m. The river fell in six hours last night 2 inches. Passed a small stream which puts into the river from the south a little above the Devil's Backbone. It heads in the hills some distance to the south of us, near a butte which we called Cap Butte, and the stream was called Gun Creek. Its valley is small, and filled with growing pine. The banks of the Yellowstone near Gun Creek are much lower than at any other point passed, so far, on the river. On the south bank we had a prairie, covered with prickly pear, sage-brush, and some bunch-grass. Hills some distance off, broken and rough. North bank closed in by range of uninviting hills, which were called North Side Buttes. Current running from four and a half to five miles an hour. At 7 a. m. we stopped at an island called Lasure's Island and wooded. Very little growing timber on the Yellowstone from Powder River up to this point, but a good deal of drift-wood scattered along the shore. Left Lasure's Island at 11 a. m., put off scouts just before leaving, and they pushed on ahead of us on the north bank. On the north side the hills, which are about 150 feet in height, close into the

Thos. G. Townsend

MOUTH OF POWDER RIVER

river just after leaving this island, and on the south side we passed a high bank of clay with coal underlying it. Joe's Island and Joe's Rapids and a small creek called Muff Creek passed about two miles beyond Lasure's Island. Hills on the south close in to the river, with plateaus on top and cedar growing on them. Prairie extending along the bank of the river on the north side of the character already described, about five miles deep. Twenty-four miles from mouth of Powder River we struck the main Buffalo Rapids, which are half a mile in length, with a current which amounts to about six miles an hour. Passed back and forth through the rapids, and found that the lowest depth of water was 7 feet in the channel. Had no trouble in steaming over them, although we had a heavy head-wind as well as the current to contend against.

In our progress up the river for the next two or three miles the surface of the water was disturbed by ripples, indicating a broken or rocky condition in the bed of the channel, which interfered with the peaceful flow of the water, but did not amount to anything like an impediment to the easy and successful navigation of the stream. We passed the mouth of Sunday Creek, which falls into the river from the north, only presenting to the eye a small valley about six miles in length; and then in succession several large and finely timbered islands, reaching the mouth of Tongue River, which is eleven miles from Sunday Creek and thirty-eight from Powder River, where we camped for the night. From the head of Buffalo Rapids, on the south bank, a high range of sharply defined hills, the most prominent butte being called Marsh's Butte, run diagonally across from the Yellowstone to the valley of the Tongue River. Between this range, which is from 200 to 300 feet high, with very little timber or verdure visible, and the two rivers, is a bottom, covered with sage, prickly pear, and bunch-grass. Along the Yellowstone the cottonwood timber increases at each step of the route till you reach the rich timbered bottom of the immediate valley of the Tongue River. On the west side of this last-named river the cottonwood fringes the Yellowstone, and behind it, running back to the hills, we found a bottom five miles long and two or more miles deep, covered as the one just described on the east bank.

*Monday, May* 31, 1875.—Left camp at the mouth of Tongue River at 3.45 a. m., and reached the mouth of the Big Horn River, which is one hundred and sixty-five miles from Powder River, and one hundred and twenty-seven miles from Tongue River, at 8.15 a. m., Wednesday, June 2.

We found the general character of the country on the north bank as described by General Stanley in his report. The only streams that we discovered flowing into the Yellowstone on the south bank, between Tongue River and the Big Horn, were Emmel's Creek and a creek which I called Alkali Creek. The former is twenty-four and a half miles, and the latter one hundred and three miles from Tongue River.

The quantity and quality of growing timber, pine and cottonwood, increased very rapidly as we made our progress to the west. The river was filled with islands, all well covered with a heavy growth of cottonwood, and the surface of the ground carpeted with fine bunch-grass, wild rye, and sage. The hills that open and shut off the valley are as a general thing not so high as those in the lower part of the river, and are rounded off, covered with sage and bunch-grass, and with every indication of a plateau country behind them which would give good grazing. Where the hills break abruptly on the river, they give sandstone bluffs instead of the clay of the lower country. The major part of the prairie-bottoms are on the north side. The only large one between the points named on the south bank runs up to within eleven miles of the Big Horn, and has a frontage on the river of about twenty-one miles, varying in width from half a mile to four miles. These prairie-bottoms are formed in two benches, the lower one from 3 to 4 feet above the water, well timbered, but by the drift-wood seen must be subject at times to an overflow; the other, or second bench, is some 4 feet higher than the first, and gradually slopes back to the hills.

After making an examination of the Big Horn we pushed on up the Yellowstone River, leaving the mouth of the former at 2.50 p. m., Wednesday, June 2, and continued to work our way onward until Monday, June 7. Above the Big Horn the water of the Yellowstone was clear; and although we left this large tributary, which is 150 yards wide and throws into the Yellowstone an immense volume of water behind us, still the channel and quantity of water and bed of the stream gave no signs, to be discovered by our eyes, of any diminution in its capacity, power, or strength. The width of the river averaged about 300 yards, and at many places, from main shore to main shore, it was fully 1,000 yards. The current of the stream increased by degrees as we got farther advanced toward its head, but our trouble did not begin until 9.25 a. m. on the 3d of June, at a place on the river called "The Narrows," twenty-seven miles above the Big Horn. At this point the bluffs on the south bank terminate, and the bluffs on the north side closing in, thus confining the river in a narrow and deep channel which is only 85 yards wide. The current was so swift near this point that we only made one-sixth of a mile an hour, and here the boat, although under a full head of steam, appeared to stand still. It was estimated that the water was running against us at this place at the rate of eight or nine miles an hour, which was much more rapid than at any other point heretofore reached on the trip. We had to use our spars and lines to-day for the first time, and succeeded in reaching and tying up for the night at Pompey's Pillar, at 5.30 p. m., June 3, 1875, thirty-nine miles from the Big Horn.

*Tuesday, June* 4, 1875.—We started from our camp at Pompey's Pillar at 3.45 a. m., and continued to fight our way forward up this mighty and swift-running stream. At times we thought that at last we had reached a point where we could put away our spars, stop our nigger-engine, and coil up our ropes, but all these dreams and hopes were blighted, for the current increased in rapidity, the river-bed continued to be broken and divided by islands, and after closing the day, June 6, with our boat fastened up for the night above Hell Roaring Rapids, and a line stretched to help us forward at early morning, it did not much surprise me to find that the developments of the next morning warranted us in deciding to retrace our steps. Upon a careful examination of the river, on the morning of the 7th of June, above us for some miles, it was ascertained that, though the volume of water was unchanged, it was so cut up into various chutes and channels, by islands, and the river-bed was so wide, with a most powerful current hurling it forward to its mouth, that any farther progress made up the stream could only be accomplished by sparring and warping, and without any adequate reward for the labor expended. So that at 2.10 p. m., June 7, we turned the prow of our boat down the river, having reached a point which we estimated to be two hundred and fifty miles above the mouth of Powder River.

I can say of the country generally that the north bank is almost continuous bluffs and hills from the Big Horn River to the large prairie opposite the mouth of Clark's Fork, and that on the south bank you have the prairie-bottom complementary thereto. Pompey's Pillar prairie

MOUTH OF BIG-HORN RIVER.

THE TURRETS or
CASTLE ROCKS YELLOWSTONE RIVER,
From South West.

is fully twenty miles long, and the prairie opposite Clark's Fork extends to the west up to, if not beyond, Bidger's Cañon. These prairies seemed to improve somewhat as we went west, though the growth was about the same as upon those already described. Growing timber along the rivers was not so abundant beyond Pompey's Pillar as up to that point, though there is an inexhaustible supply in the country to meet all the demands that a settlement of this valley would require.

In regard to the rivers rising south of the Yellowstone and emptying into it, I shall first mention Tongue River. The water of this river is of a reddish tinge. It is 150 feet wide at its mouth, and holds to this width for some two miles or more from the main river. It is quite crooked, with a depth of water at mouth of 7 feet.

The main valley of the Yellowstone is about two miles wide where it is joined by the above stream, and is a prairie-bottom with some good grazing. Both streams are well timbered with cottonwood, and where the Tongue River breaks through the hills its valley is about two miles wide. The hills on the east bank are 350 feet high, and the country beyond is very broken. Those on the north near the main valley are clear cut, conical in shape, covered with sage-brush and bunch-grass, and are not over 150 feet high, but increase as you go up the valley.

## ROSEBUD RIVER.

I found the place where this river was reported as emptying into the Yellowstone, but the bed of the stream which I examined was a dry one, with no signs of water. The valley where it joins the Yellowstone is not over a mile long, all told, and no signs of any camps or occupation by Indians; very little timber and no valley to it except the short one from hills of Yellowstone to the main river. In fact, the result of my examination, both going up and coming down the Yellowstone, leads me to believe that the Rosebud River does not empty into the Yellowstone direct, but that its waters are conveyed to it through the Tongue River; that is, I think that it empties into the Tongue River and not into the Yellowstone.

*Emmel's Creek* is twenty-four and a half miles above Tongue River, about 25 or 30 feet wide, and winds its way through a small prairie from the hills to the parent stream; has some cottonwood and ash growing on its banks. Near its mouth we found four piles of stone, which mark the point where Meldrum's trading-post once stood. Signs of old Indian camps near this stream.

*Alkali Creek* finds its way down to the Yellowstone through a large prairie below the mouth of the Big Horn River, and at a distance from Tongue River estimated to be one hundred and three miles. It has a fringe of cottonwood-trees on its banks, is about fifteen or twenty feet wide, water alkali, and of a reddish tinge. Signs of Indian camps near its mouth in the main valley.

## THE BIG HORN RIVER.

We steamed up this river for a distance of twelve miles, found it quite crooked, with a narrow valley, and were obliged to return on account of the water becoming distributed over so wide a space that the main channel did not afford sufficient depth of water for us to continue our course. The current of the Big Horn was about as strong as that of the Yellowstone, water muddy, and at the mouth it was about 150 yards wide. Where it joins the Yellowstone the points of land on each side are small prairies, with good grass. On the east bank the bluffs run close to the river and are sparsely timbered. On the west bank the valley is mostly filled with cottonwood, and the hills are about 150 feet high, with plateaus on their top. Near the point where we turned back, there was a small stretch of prairie about a mile wide and a mile and a half long. The north bank of the Yellowstone opposite the mouth of the river is a sandstone bluff 150 feet high, with rolling plateau on top, covered with sage and some bunch-grass.

### PRYOR'S RIVER.

Where this stream empties into the Yellowstone sixty-two miles above the Big Horn, it is a small creek 25 feet wide, winding through the western part of the prairie which extends from Pompey's Pillar to it; very little timber on it. It is reported to have a fine country near its head-waters.

We entered the mouth of the Yellowstone River at 6½ p. m., Wednesday, May 27th, and returned to Fort Buford on Thursday, June 10. Our running-time from Fort Buford to the mouth of the Big Horn, under steam alone, was 88 hours and 40 minutes. From the time that we arrived at the mouth of Powder River, Sunday, May 30, up to the 7th day of June, the river fell from half an inch to one and a half inches each night, and the water in the channel was over two feet below the ordinary high-water mark. The Yellowstone River, from the highest point reached by us to the mouth of Powder River, sweeps through the country in long and majestic stretches, with a current of at least four miles an hour. Its bosom is studded with islands by hundreds, some of which are three or more miles in length, and covered with cottonwood groves; and many of them are so handsome that they almost make the voyager believe that they are the well-kept grounds pertaining to some English country-house. I never saw so fine a growth of cottonwood in my life as on the Yellowstone twenty-five miles above Tongue River. These trees will run from 3 to 5 feet, and some are 6 feet in diameter. The supply of cottonwood and pine which exists throughout the Upper Yellowstone country is ample to meet all the requirements of any settlement of the valley; and the indications are that large beds of coal can be found and worked in the neighborhood of Powder River. Sandstone bluffs crop out on the Yellowstone above Tongue River, and some limestone was passed above Pompey's Pillar.

The mouth of the Big Horn may be regarded as the head of navigation on the Yellowstone River, and for three months of the year this river presents less obstacles to its navigation than the Upper Missouri, and, indeed, many other rivers in this and other countries. The channel is unchanging, for it passes over a gravel bed from its head to its mouth, and there are no snags. When this is contrasted with the shifting and unreliable water of the Upper Missouri, it ought to make the rates of insurance less on the Yellowstone River than on the Upper Missouri.

### GAME.

We found the greatest abundance of game along our entire route—antelope, bear, black-tail deer, elk, mountain sheep; also herds of buffalo between Tongue River and the Big Horn as we went up, but before we returned they had all crossed the river and gone north.

### INDIANS.

On the north bank of the Yellowstone River, about eight miles above the mouth of Pryor's River, we ran on to a camp of Mountain Crow-

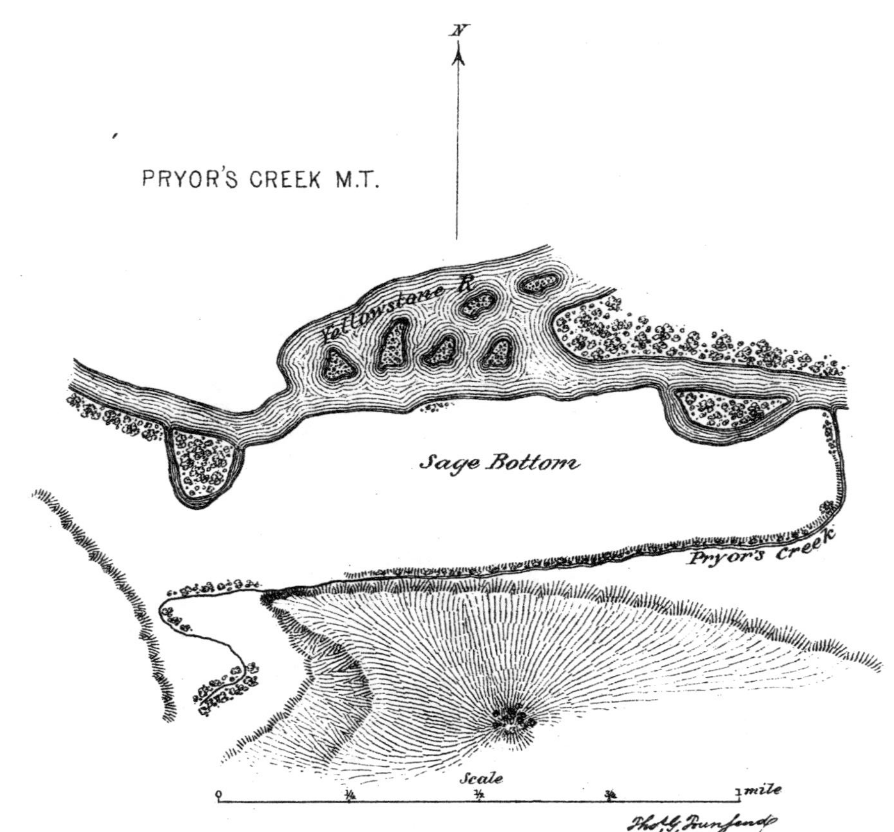
PRYOR'S CREEK M.T.
N
Yellowstone R.
Sage Bottom
Pryor's Creek
Scale
0
1/4
1/2
3/4
1 mile

Indians, on their way down to the Big Porcupine to hunt. This camp consisted of 270 lodges of Mountain Crows, under Iron Bull, Black Foot, Crazy Head, Long Horse, and Bear Wolf; 50 lodges of Nez Percés, under Looking Glass; 20 lodges River Crows, under Black Bull and Forked Tail; 10 lodges of Gros Ventres of the Prairie, under Brass Bracelet; 1 lodge of Bannacks; making in all 351 lodges. They had their families with them and large herds of horses. I was told that these Indians had above 15,000 rounds of carbine ammunition, which they were supplied with by the Indian Bureau, and they boasted that if they could only get a chance at Sitting Bull and his people, they would not leave one of them to tell the tale of their meeting. They said that the Big Horn country belonged to them and they intended to have it, if they had to kill all the Sioux Nation. Most of these Indians were armed with Sharp's carbines.

No Sioux were seen at any time during the expedition.

I learned while in the Crow camp that their agency had been transferred from the vicinity of Fort Ellis to the wagon-road crossing of the Big Rosebud.

The following table of distances was estimated and compiled on our way up, and verified on our way down the river:

## DISTANCES.

*Distances (local and total) on the Yellowstone River, above the mouth of Powder River, estimated by a comparison of those taken while ascending and descending.*

| | Local. | Total. |
|---|---|---|
| | *Miles.* | *Miles.* |
| Mouth of Powder River to Bear Rapids | 5 | 5 |
| Devil's Backbone | 7 | 12 |
| Main Buffalo Rapids | 12 | 24 |
| Sunday Creek | 3 | 27 |
| Reynold's Island | 2 | 29 |
| Tongue River | 9 | 38 |
| General Custer's first fight, (scene of) | 11 | 49 |
| Poncie Island | 14 | 63 |
| Little Porcupine | 6 | 69 |
| Emmel's Creek | 3½ | 72½ |
| Big Porcupine | 5½ | 78 |
| Avenue Island, (Bessie Butte) | 3 | 81 |
| Bear Island | 2 | 83 |
| Palisades | 27 | 110 |
| Alkali Creek | 31 | 141 |
| Scene of General Custer's fight | 22 | 163 |
| Big Horn River | 2 | 165 |
| Cape Horn | 10 | 175 |
| The Narrows | 17 | 192 |
| Pompey's Pillar | 12 | 204 |
| Pryor's Creek | 23 | 227 |
| Highest Point | 23 | 250 |

Gen. George A. Forsyth, in his report of May, 1873, makes the distance from Fort Buford to mouth of Powder River two hundred and thirty-five miles. I am of the opinion that this is too great. By the system adopted by us in estimating the distance traveled, we made it one hundred and eighty miles from Fort Buford to the mouth of Powder River.

I am under many obligations to Lieut. Richard E. Thompson, Sixth

Infantry, for his assistance during the expedition, and for the map which I herewith forward. The pen sketches of the country transmitted were made by Lieut. T. G. Townsend, Sixth Infantry, and presented to me for file with this report; and the book of pencil-views was made by Corporal Thoma, Sixth Infantry.

Very respectfully, your obedient servant,

JAMES W. FORSYTH,
*Lieutenant-Colonel and Military Secretary.*

Lieut. Gen. P. H. SHERIDAN,
*Commanding Military Division of the Missouri.*

# REPORT OF LIEUT. COL. F. D. GRANT.

HEADQUARTERS MILITARY DIVISION OF THE MISSOURI,
*Chicago, Ill., June* 23, 1875.

GENERAL: I have the honor to submit the following report of my observations on my recent trip up the Yellowstone River, in obedience to Special Orders No. 54, dated Headquarters Military Division of the Missouri, Chicago, Ill., May 19, 1875.

I left Chicago and went to Saint Paul; thence, via the Northern Pacific Railroad, to Bismarck, Dakota Territory, where the steamer Josephine was waiting for us. We took this steamer, which was to take us up the Yellowstone and Missouri Rivers, stopping at Forts Stevenson and Buford. At these two points we took on our escort. At Fort Stevenson we took one company of forty men and one Gatling gun; at Fort Buford, sixty men. We entered the mouth of the Yellowstone on the evening of May 26, and ran up the river until 8.20 p. m., when we stopped to cut wood for the next day's run. As no white person lives on the Yellowstone River, we had to cut all the wood used on this expedition.

Our first day's run took us up the river to Forsyth's Buttes, about twelve miles. We proceeded up the river until the afternoon of June 7, when we found the river so cut up with islands, and all the chutes having rapids, that it was practically the head of navigation, and decided to return, as the object of the expedition had been accomplished.

The distance of the highest point reached from the mouth of Powder River we estimated as two hundred and forty-eight miles. The distance from the mouth of the Powder River to the mouth of the Yellowstone had been estimated by the expedition of 1873 as two hundred and thirty-five miles, making a total distance of four hundred and eighty-three miles.

In writing this report, I think I shall treat each subject in succession, rather than taking them as we passed up the river, as there was very little variation from day to day.

## THE COUNTRY.

The country we passed through was of a cretaceous formation, (the latest formations of the Mesozoic times, going up through Cenozoic time and the age of man, for the country is being severely washed by the heavy rains of the present day;) the valley, of course, being, like the valleys of all rivers, modified drift. The islands, of which there are a great many, differ from those of the Missouri in being comparatively permanent.

The Yellowstone Valley presents many beautiful landscapes. It is particularly grand when seen from the mouth of Powder River; but from the mouth of this river down the soil is an ashy clay, on which little or nothing will grow. Adjoining the river, however, are several extensive flats, which are comparatively fertile. There is a sort of coal (lignite) in all the banks below Powder River, but very little stone of any sort, except sandstone of the very poorest quality. The coal found here will make a very hot fire, but contains so much sulphur that I doubt that it could ever be used for anything except to be burnt in an open grate to keep a room warm.

In 1873, when I was out in this country, I found fossils of several kinds, shells, leaves of fern, and the backbone of some sort of animal; I do not know what.

The clay of this country must contain considerable lime, for wherever these beds of coal have been burnt out, there is always just above where the coal was, a bed of gypsum, (sulphate of lime,) and above this red banks. All the ravines in these hills have cedar in small quantity, which could be used by actual settlers for doors, window-sills, &c., but not enough to send to a market, even if there was one nearer than it is likely there will ever be to this part of the river.

From Powder River up, sandstone makes it appearance in larger quantities, and the hills are capped with gravel mixed with earth 8 to 10 feet thick, and on these bluffs or hills there is a thin growth of grass and pine trees until you get up to the Big Horn River.

From here up the hills are much higher, the sandstone much harder and in thicker strata. The growth of pine is much larger and more of them. Judging from the game, (buffalo,) there must be twenty or thirty miles back from the river a park country, on the south side of the river, for the buffalo were coming from that direction, crossing the river and going north.

Also we could see high snow-capped mountains in the distance, and I have always found that the foot-hills of a mountain-range are good lands.

I have heard hunters who have been through this country say that colors of gold have been found in the different streams coming out of these mountains, and I know that the gold-mines in Montana are in the same range. I also know that the Yellowstone River and its various tributaries coming from these mountains have a gravelly bottom of igneous and metamorphic rocks, porphyry, granite, and quartz; so I see no reason that there should not be gold, even in considerable quantities, in these mountains.

## THE YELLOWSTONE RIVER.

This river has its source in the Yellowstone Lake, (which is in the northwestern corner of Wyoming Territory,) and takes a course a little west of north, until it unites its waters with those of Shield's River. At this point it turns and runs in a general direction a little north of east, until the Powder River empties into it, when it changes again and takes an almost due northeastern course, emptying into the Missouri River a few miles above Fort Buford.

In low water this stream is navigable with ease as far up as Pompey's Pillar, (a sandstone bluff situated on the south side, and cut off from a range of sandstone hills on the north by the action of water,) about thirty miles above the mouth of the Big Horn River, there being but one place from its mouth to this point that would have to be fixed to improve its navigation. A couple of bowlders would have to be removed from near the mouth of the Powder River. These bowlders could be removed by three or four men in a few hours by drilling holes and blowing them up. The only other obstacles in the way are the different rapids. Most of these a steamboat can run over without any trouble. Some are almost too rapid, and those can be cordelled without any trouble. To cordelle is to tie a long rope around a tree or stump on shore, and the other end wrapped around the capstan of the boat, which is turned by steam, and thus the boat is pulled along.

There are large quantities of dry wood along the river that has been cut by the beaver. This makes it very easy for steamboats for fuel should they ever begin to navigate this river.

## DISTANCES.

The following are the names of the places and distances on the Yellowstone. I give the names of only those above the mouth of Powder River, as those below that point have already been given in a report of Gen. G. A. Forsyth, in 1873.

| Names. | Remarks. | Local distance. | Distance from mouth of Powder River. | Distance from mouth of Yellowstone. |
|---|---|---|---|---|
| Mouth of Yellowstone | | | | |
| Powder River | | 235 | 0 | 235 |
| Bear Rapids | Very swift current | 5 | 5 | 240 |
| Devil's Backbone | Left bank, opposite Gun Creek | 7 | 12 | 247 |
| Buffalo Rapids | As formidable as any in the river | 12 | 24 | 259 |
| Sunday Creek | Left bank | 3 | 27 | 262 |
| Reynold's Island | Right bank | 2 | 29 | 264 |
| Tongue River | Right bank, good site for post | 8 | 37 | 272 |
| Scene of Custer's first fight, 1873 | Left bank | 11 | 48 | 283 |
| Poncie Island | Right bank | 14 | 62 | 297 |
| Little Porcupine River | Left bank | 6 | 68 | 303 |
| Emmel's Creek | Right bank, Meldrum's trading post | 3½ | 71½ | 306½ |
| Big Porcupine | Right bank, good site for post | 5½ | 77 | 312 |
| Avenue Island | | 3 | 80 | 315 |
| Bear Island | Of considerable size; bear seen on it | 2 | 82 | 317 |
| Palisades | A range of sandstone bluffs, left bank | 27 | 109 | 344 |
| Alkali Creek | Right bank | 31 | 140 | 375 |
| Scene of Custer's second fight | Left bank; fought in 1873 | 22 | 162 | 397 |
| Big Horn River | Volume of water about one-third of Yellowstone | 2 | 164 | 399 |
| Cape Horn | A very sharp bend of the river | 10 | 174 | 409 |
| The Narrows | About 75 or 80 yards wide | 17 | 191 | 426 |
| Pompey's Pillar | About 150 feet high, right bank | 12 | 203 | 438 |
| Little Grant Rapids | Very strong current | 15 | 218 | 453 |
| Pryor's Creek | Right bank | 8 | 226 | 461 |
| Belle Buttes | Right bank, Hell Gate Rapids here | 10 | 236 | 471 |
| Highest point reached | | 12 | 248 | 483 |

If a military post is to be established on the Yellowstone, I would respectfully recommend the mouth of Tongue River as the point to locate it. Tongue River runs through the very heart of the country inhabited by hostile Indians, and is, therefore, in my opinion, the best place for a post.

The water of the Yellowstone is deeper than that of the Missouri above the mouth of the Yellowstone, and could be navigated more months in the year than the Missouri can be. The distance from its mouth to the head of navigation is about one-half the distance from the mouth of the Yellowstone to Fort Benton, and the distance from Pompey's Pillar to the settled part of Montana is about the same distance as it is from Fort Benton, and I believe a good wagon-road all the way could be had by following the Yellowstone up to Crow agency, and then going across to the Gallatin Valley.

## THE ISLANDS.

The islands of this river, like those of the Missouri, are all modified drift, finely timbered with cottonwood, box-elder, and near the mouth of the river some ash. These islands are, however, more permanent than any in the Missouri, inasmuch as their foundations are gravel, and do not wash away. Some of them are very large, and there are a great many of them.

### FISH.

The fish of this river are catfish, caught near the mouth; shiners, catfish, and jack-salmon between Powder River and the Big Horn. Above the mouth of the Big Horn we caught trout, catfish, and shiners.

### GAME.

The game found on this trip was buffalo, (between the Powder and Big Horn Rivers,) elk in great number on the islands, beaver on all the banks, antelope on the plains, big-horn or mountain sheep in the bluffs, wild geese and ducks, which breed here in great numbers. We saw a few bears and a few wolves.

### INDIANS.

This is the hunting-ground of the hostile Sioux, who roam at large between the Powder River and the Big Horn, on the south side of the river, and between the Yellowstone and the Musselshell on the north. The Crow Indians live west of the Big Horn River.

### THE RESOURCES OF THE COUNTRY.

The Yellowstone valley can all or nearly all be cultivated, as the soil is rich. The islands, many of which are very large, could also be cultivated. There is an abundance of coal and pine wood that could be taken out with profit. The water is fine, being melted snow, and in the valley there grow large quantities of wild plums, cherries, buffalo-berries, gooseberries, currants, and wild strawberries.

I am, general, very respectfully, your obedient servant,

F. D. GRANT,
*Lieutenant-Colonel and Aide-de-Camp.*

Lieut. Gen. P. H. SHERIDAN,
*Commanding Military Division of the Missouri.*

## INDORSEMENTS ON REPORT.

[First Indorsement.]

HEADQUARTERS MILITARY DIVISION MISSOURI,
*Chicago, June* 30, 1875.

Respectfully forwarded to the Headquarters of the Army.

P. H. SHERIDAN,
*Lieutenant-General Commanding.*

---

[Second Indorsement.]

HEADQUARTERS OF THE ARMY,
*Saint Louis, July* 7, 1875.

Respectfully forwarded to the Secretary of War.

W. T. SHERMAN,
*General.*

---

[Third Indorsement.]

WAR DEPARTMENT, ADJUTANT-GENERAL'S OFFICE,
*Washington, July* 9, 1875.

Respectfully submitted to the Secretary of War.

THOMAS M. VINCENT,
*Assistant Adjutant-General.*

---

Respectfully referred to the Chief of Engineers.

The Secretary of War directs that this report be published, under the supervision of the Chief of Engineers, at the Government Printing-Office.

By order of the Secretary of War.

H. T. CROSBY,
*Chief Clerk.*

WAR DEPARTMENT,
*September* 15, 1875.

www.ingramcontent.com/pod-product-compliance
Lightning Source LLC
LaVergne TN
LVHW011141110826
845150LV00008B/2453

* 9 7 8 1 4 1 8 1 9 2 5 8 7 *